D1410465

QUIET THOUGHTS

Paul S. McElroy

Illustrations by Stanley Clough

PETER PAUPER PRESS
Mount Vernon, New York

Every generation enjoys the use of a vast hoard bequeathed to it by antiquity, and transmits that hoard, augmented by fresh acquisitions to future ages.

THOMAS MACAULAY

We have been careful that they that will read may have delight, and they that are desirous to commit to memory might have ease, and that all into whose hands it come might profit.

II MACCABEES 2:25

WHEN?

WHEN is the prime of life? At the peak of physical prowess? At the height of intellectual attainment? At the moment of greatest maturity? At the end of long years? Who can say when death is premature? Does it come too late for one who is helplessly invalided or tortured by pain incurable? Does death come too late for a Methuselah? Is long life a reward for good behavior? Does death come too soon for one who gives his life that others may be spared? Too soon for the hero and adventurer? Does early death come as punishment for misdeeds? Why should death be feared? All men must face what is inevitable. Man begins to die as soon as he is born. At what moment, then, should man be most fearful of leaving the known for the unknown? Understandably there may be a desire to postpone the transition, but what is there to be afraid of? Why should one be sad or rebellious? Does not one look with anticipation toward each tomorrow? When the time comes for departure shall not the man of faith also look forward trustingly and with eager curiosity to what the new adventure may bring?

INDECISION

THERE is probably more harm resulting from the lack of decision than from the wrong decision. The secret is to distinguish between the inability to make a decision and the wisdom of waiting for new evidence. In some circumstances a decision cannot be given at the moment, but in many instances it is possible and advantageous to make up our minds one way or the other more promptly than we do. As Shakespeare said, "If 'twere done, when 'twere done, then 'twere well it were done quickly." The postponement of a decision for the sake of further study is desirable, but sheer procrastination needlessly delays action and invites frustration.

NEEDLESS BURDENS

NOTHING burdens or weights us down so needlessly as does some grudge or resentment held against another. Usually resentments grow out of misunderstandings or from unwillingness to face honestly some disagreeable or embarrassing situation. Opposite conclusions are frequently drawn by two people from the same set of circumstances. Oftentimes opponents do not differ so much in their aims or objectives as in their methods. Therefore, it is well to remove the areas of disagreement rather than to build up walls of prejudice. It is surprising how quickly resentment is removed when we try to recall the good things that may be said about our adversary.

THE EDUCATED HEART

REAL gratitude, like joy, is a feeling, a spirit, an attitude that cannot be concealed. It has to be expressed. It is more than lip service, more than a polite, perfunctory "Thank you," said in return for a favor. Scripture tells of ten lepers being cleansed but only one returning to give thanks. One wonders if contemporary ingratitude is as high as ninety percent. Too many fail to express their appreciation in any way. Some people have had so much done for them that in their eager expectation they become demanding when more is not forthcoming. Such people have not learned to be grateful. Their heart has not been educated to the point where they become consciously and constantly aware of their indebtedness to others. The first step toward educating the heart is deliberately and regularly to express appreciation to others. A second step is to give praise or thanks to God from whom all blessings flow.

"Count your many blessings, name them
one by one,
And it will surprise you what the Lord
has done."

The one whose heart is educated will join with the Psalmist and say, "Bless the Lord, O my soul, and all that is within me, bless His holy name. Bless the Lord and forget not all His benefits." This is the essence of gratitude.

CHAIN RE-ACTION

WHATEVER we do or fail to do and say has such subtle and far-reaching influence that we can never tell what the result will be. Our shadows fall where we may never be. A deed or word may set in motion forces that change the history of the world. Even our reactions to what is said and done help or hinder the prog-

ress of the world by just so much. So interdependent are we that we are dependent upon each other and one deed depends upon another. Our present thinking and circumstances have been determined by a series of previous decisions. The hope of flying, for instance, was long in the hearts of men, dating back to the myth of Daedalus and the waxen wings which melted in the hot sun, before aviation became a reality. Man did not actually fly until a series of discoveries and inventions had been made, each dependent upon knowledge gained by previous ones. Similarly in other realms, as Confucius pointed out: When the heart is set aright, the personal life is cultivated. When the personal life is cultivated, then the family is regulated. When the family is regulated, the national life is orderly. When the national life is orderly, then there is peace in the world.

WORSHIP

WORSHIP is important and difficult. It is an attempt to make clear the reality and nearness of God to the end that God may be able to do for us, in us, and through us, and so for the world-at-large, what He desires. That is why the greatest discoveries yet to be made will be along spiritual lines and by means of worship. The more meaningful worship becomes the more clearly will we realize that material things do not bring happiness and are of little value in making us more creatively powerful. Whether worship be expressed in private prayer or in corporate observance, it involves the whole of life.

THE GREAT ADVENTURE

THE longer we live the stronger the ties become which attract us toward another world, and the fewer and the weaker those that attach us to this. In journeys during life we move from one place to another with reluctance to leave the old, but so eager are we for the new that we cannot be held back. So with the Great Adventure there may be reluctance to take our final farewell, but there comes a time when there is such eagerness to move on that we would not permit ourselves to be held back, even if we could. We enjoy our work, our home, our friends, our life, and we shall be sorry to part with all that is so dear to us; but when the time comes we can look "forward with eager curiosity and glad hopefulness to the new world to which the unknown voyage will bring us." All through life we have accepted God's gifts of love and mercy. Surely One who has provided for us in life beyond what we could ask or pray will not desert us as we move from one world to another. With Socrates we ought to be "of good cheer in the face of death and to hold firmly that this one thing, at least, is true: no evil can come to a righteous man either in life or in death, and his interests are not neglected by the gods."

INSTRUMENTS OF DESTINY

THE great events of history have evolved around some personality. In times of great national stress it seems nothing short of providential that certain people have been found in certain places at certain times with certain qualifications. It is as though certain people were born for such times. Many of the things we do have such far-reaching results that we may not realize the part we play in the process, but to the extent that we influence history we are instruments of destiny. When King Xerxes summoned his wife to a huge, gala banquet, she refused to attend. It became a matter of court importance, for her defiance was a threat to the supremacy of the king. His advisors pressed for divorce and the adopted daughter of Mordecai, Esther, was made queen, and Mordecai himself was made chamberlain. Esther disclosed a plot to kill all the Jews and assassinate King Xerxes. Because Esther was queen she was able to spare her people from disaster but there was real danger that she herself might not survive when her real identity as a Jewess was discovered. When Mordecai, mindful of the unique position Esther held in the destiny of her people, urged her to reveal the plot to the king, he challenged her with the haunting question which now lays claim upon us: "Who knows but you were born for such a time as this?"

SUFFERING: TRAGEDY OR VICTORY?

There are times when a man cares for nothing but the cessation of his pain. It sometimes seems as if his pain were carried to an extreme and unendurable limit. He turns from it in horror, regards it as useless, and even accuses God of cruelty because the suffering is so intense.

> *"When sickness comes and bids us rest*
> *awhile*
> *In some calm pool, beside life's too swift*
> *stream,*
> *Why rail at Fate, and count ourselves ill*
> *used?*
> *'Tis then one's soul awakes, weaves dream*
> *on dream."*

Those who have reached the depths claim suffering can be one of the most wonderful experiences of life. It can make us or break us — depending upon how we take it. We can make of it a beacon to light the world and give strength to posterity. Through example, we can demonstrate to others the nobility of a disciplined and undefeated courage. Can we not trust that somehow good will be the final outcome of evil?

JUSTICE PLUS

ANYONE charged with executing justice will seek to have the punishment fit the crime. So long as it is possible to exert retribution then justice seems to be fulfilled, but the doctrine of an eye for an eye and a tooth for a tooth lacks creativity and seldom solves the problem. No matter how equitable the penalty, justice usually leaves the defendant and the plaintiff unsatisfied and with hurt feelings. Love is more comprehensive than justice. Love is not some sentimental emotion which disregards justice. Love does not mean to feel for others an emotion such as one experiences for a wife, or sister or father. Love is based on justice, but it also demands the well-being of all concerned. Love does not mean doing away with justice or by-passing punishment. It neither ignores the offense nor rejects the offender. Love stands by and seeks to heal and restore a right relationship between men and with God.

THE FAULT IS WITHIN

How easy it is to blame others for our failures! No doubt others often make it difficult for us to succeed, but to blame our defeat on others is really to admit that we ourselves are not big enough to overcome the obstacles that are in the way. When the expert misses the mark he looks for the fault within himself. Failure to hit the bull's eye, or to reach the goal, is not so much the fault of something beyond ourselves as of something within ourselves. To improve our aim we must improve ourselves. To succeed we must overcome the difficulties and not be overcome by them, for obstacles are but a challenge to the person determined to win. Of many a situation it has been said, "It can't be done," but of every achievement made against insurmountable odds it can be said, "It couldn't be done, but somehow it was done."

THE FREE MAN

UNLESS a person can control his passions, his desires, and his fears he is not in possession of himself. No man is free who is not in command of himself. Since a man's worth is measured not in terms of what he does or what he has, but what he is, it is desirable for us to become masters of ourselves. This means that we must be inner directed, motivated by convictions rather than pushed about, like a weathervane, by pres-

sures from without. This ability to act in accord with our convictions, to do what we ought and want to do and not as someone else wants us to do, is to be free.

SORROW AND JOY

SORROW and joy are yoked together not for contrast but because they are different expressions of the same physiological condition — excessive emotional tension! They are twin foci around which emotions revolve. It is a fallacy to assume that sorrow implies evil and that joy represents happiness, for even in laughter the heart is sad and the end of joy is heaviness. Love, which is part of joy, is so wrapped up with grief that we would not want our grief taken from us, even if it could be. Legend tells of the woman who came to the river Styx to be ferried across to the land of departed spirits. Charos, the ferryman, offers her a certain potion which can cause her to forget the life she is leaving and all of its sorrows. In the end, the woman leaves the draught untasted choosing to remember life's pains and sorrows and failures rather than to forget its joys, its triumphs and its loves. Sorrow and joy belong together. They are precious experiences which deepen understanding and give meaning to life.

BELONGING

I, MY, ME, and MINE are possessive words used to describe what we feel belongs to us. Actually, much that we claim is not ours at all. In the last analysis we can claim not what is given to us but only what we give away. There is truth in the words:

> "What I had I saved.
> What I saved I lost.
> What I gave I have."

What belongs to us is not as important as to what we belong. There is unconquerable strength in being identified with some worthy cause and in belonging to some purposeful group. Without some such identification we flounder like a ship without a rudder. We keep going but lack direction. That to which we belong and to which we give our allegiance and loyalty must be worthy and should represent the highest and the very best that we know.

LIVING WITH OTHERS

We MUST live with those whose manners annoy us, whose practices offend us, and whose ideas disturb us. We must somehow learn to get along with these people or else be forever at odds with them, with ourselves, and with the world. Our tendency is to build a wall that will shut out those who differ from us, but each time we erect a barrier to shut someone out, we also shut ourselves in. We must remember that no matter what minority interest we may choose to safeguard, we are at the same time members of a larger society and these larger and more inclusive loyalties must be preserved. It is not wise to exalt our particular minority interest to the exclusion of the larger loyalty. The part is never greater than the whole. It is well to let the things for which we stand win their way into the hearts of others through their own merit, to let causes and issues grow in strength through their own inherent goodness, rather than trying to wall them out because of our own lack of understanding, jealousy, pride or prejudice. To live with others we need to see the situation from the other person's point of view.

THE INDISPENSABLE

THE word love is greatly overworked and terribly misused, often connoting expressions from orgies to bliss. The Greeks make a distinction in kinds of love. *Charos* or charity means to have a common concern for others. *Agapé* signifies primarily a voluntary, active affection such as a spiritual quality that links God and man and unites soul with soul in divine communion. *Philias* implies a social love, a filial relationship or friendship. *Eros* is used to describe sexual or erotic love. *Storgi* designates the kind of relationship or love that is found in the family and in natural affection. True love involves loyalty. Loyalty is love with a plus. Loyalty is *philias* that is strong enough to hold people together under any circumstances. This kind of love has been described as being "patient and kind . . . not jealous or boastful; . . . not arrogant or rude . . . does not insist on its own way; . . . is not irritable or resentful . . .

does not rejoice at wrong, but rejoices in the
right . . . bears all things, believes all things,
hopes all things." (I Corinthians 13:4-7, RSV)

FACE INTO THE GALE

THE experienced sailor knows that a vessel
must head into a storm to avoid shipwreck. He
must keep the ship facing into the gale. It takes
courage to head seemingly into further trouble,
but it is only by facing difficulties that they can
be conquered. There are some things that cannot be avoided and which, if not resisted, will
overcome and overwhelm us. The difficulty with
trying to run away from an adversary is that
an adversary, like the wind, runs faster, soon
catches up and overcomes all in its wake. The
wise man never turns his back on trouble, he
faces it, and in so doing becomes a victor instead
of a victim.

NOTHING IS UNIMPORTANT

WHAT we do may seem of little importance to
us, but every act, word and decision helps or
hinders the progress of the world by just so

much. It takes only a little leaven to ferment the whole lump. All too often we judge the importance of anything by the way it affects us, but what seems important to us may be unimportant in God's sight, and conversely, what is unimportant to us may be very important in God's sight. We can not always tell, when we act, just what the result will be. Our vision, our interests, our standards of value may be quite different from God's. That is why we should seek to do only those things which we think are pleasing in His sight.

THE FELLOWSHIP OF THOSE WHO CARE

How grateful we are for churches, hospitals, museums, symphonies and civic centers — to mention only a few of the philanthropic endeavors which are made possible because somebody cares enough to support them. It is not irrelevant to ask whether these organizations are made possible because of us or in spite of us. Are we, as someone has suggested, part of the problem or part of the solution? The world moves forward and progress is made because there are

those who care. People who are trying to lift the level of living of those around them soon discover that they have ties which bind them together. This world-wide fellowship of those who care transcends language, color and nationality. The world moves forward because of those who build noble projects and support them.

TWO MASTERS

WE ARE often frustrated because we desire two mutually exclusive things: evil pleasures and a pure conscience, idleness and success, a selfish life and a reputation for generosity. No one can serve two masters, for either he will hate one and love the other, or he will be devoted to one and despise the other. One cannot long serve conflicting interests simultaneously. To advocate justice but deceive our neighbor is to compromise with principle for the sake of personal gain. To rationalize is an attempt to make immoral or unethical practices conform to a sensitive and troubled conscience. We cannot ride in opposite directions at the same time, we cannot straddle the fence indefinitely, we cannot serve God and mammon. Life must be integrated; this means that all our inner forces must be coordinated and subordinated to the will of God.

FIVE KEYS

In Durham Cathedral there is an ironclad, oaken chest with five locks. In olden days each of five church officers held a key to one of the five locks, and they — the bursar, almoner, sacrist, hosteler, and verger—all had to be present and in agreement before the chest could be opened. Five keys are needed to unlock many treasures today: love, patience, cooperation, worthy purpose, and willingness. The key we hold is essential for a successful venture.

SOONER OR LATER

One thing we have to face sooner or later is death, and we are better prepared if we have given some thought to it in advance. When death comes prematurely we need not feel that injustice has been done and that the deceased has been unfairly deprived of that precious element known as time — as though extra time on earth were reward for good behavior. It is the way we use our allotted time, whether it be seven or seventy years, that is important. Our bodies are lent us during our earthly existence to assist us while we are here. What a wretched world this would be without the prospect of death, if we were to survive *ad infinitum* with all our ailments and physical handicaps. We would not want to carry on forever with our youthful immaturity nor would we wish to bear forever the infirmities of old age. Death is a merciful means of getting rid of the physical body which has housed our spirit on earth. It may be compared to the discarding of the shell when the chicken is about to enter a new world.

IT ALL DEPENDS

Age is relative. It depends upon what kind of age we mean. In a progressive school a child when asked how old he was reputedly replied, "Well, the latest personal survey shows my anatomical age as seven, my psychological age as twelve, my physiological age as six, and my moral age as four. I presume, however, you refer to my chronological age which is eight."

Age does not depend upon accumulated birthdays, but upon the elasticity of our spirit and the vigor of our mind. Age is a quality of mind. If we have left our dreams behind and hope is cold, and we have ceased to look ahead, and our ambition's fires are dead, then we are old. But if from life we take the best, and if in life we keep the jest, and still hold love, then no matter how the years go by, no matter how the birthdays fly, we are not old.

HOW BIG IS YOUR GOD?

FOR some people God remains, as He was for primitive man—a jealous, revengeful and capricious power, playing favoritism instead of being a Ruler who demands justice and righteousness. There are those who still cling to the antiquated and provincial concept of a nationalistic or local, tribal deity, instead of regarding God as the one and only governor of all the universe. Many now accept the more mature concept of God as one who gives and demands love from His people as a father does from his children. God Himself remains the same, unchanged through all ages; it is only our concept of God that changes.

It makes a difference in our behavior how we think of God. The person whose God is too small will be inadequate to the demands of life. A God that is small enough for our understanding is not large enough for our needs. By searching we may never find out all about God, but it is possible and desirable for us to keep growing in our knowledge and love of God and to worship a God that is big enough for all exigencies.

THE HAND OF GOD

ON THE outskirts of the desert where village life goes along much as it did centuries ago, an eclipse of the moon occurred. As the shadow crept across the face of the moon the residents were asked what was happening. Some replied that the moon was only sinking behind a mountain; others claimed it was merely the quarter phase of the moon; still others said it was hiding behind a cloud, but one old village sheikh, undisturbed by the growing darkness, imaginatively assured the onlookers that the phenomenon was the hand of God covering the moon. To be able to see the hand of God at work in the world is one of the greatest assets one can have. When the shadows are gathering for life's darker moments, the person who can still see God's hand at work, even in unfavorable circumstances, will be master of any situation life may impose upon him.

WORRY, ANXIETY AND FEAR

ANXIETY is a signal of impending disaster and worry is the mental activity that attempts to find a way of handling the threat. Anxiety and worry, then, can be constructive forces helping us to find our way through life. In this sense our best safety lies in anxiety or fear. Fear springs from ignorance. Knowledge is an antidote to fear. Faith counteracts fear. There comes a time when we have to accept on faith the things about which we lack knowledge. Perfect love casts out fear.

THINGS DON'T JUST HAPPEN

A GREAT many things happen without any apparent reason or purpose. In fact, we often seem to be the innocent victims of capricious, cruel and impersonal forces. Even though the explanation of events is hidden, science assures us that things don't just happen. A host of factors enter into every act. Every little thing, imperceptible and insignificant though it may seem, makes its contribution. A minimum number of blows by hammer on chisel are required to split the rock, a minimum number of snowflakes must melt before the ground is cooled enough to let others lodge unharmed. So, too, myriad deeds are required to make possible each great event in history. Our littlest effort helps make great things possible.

THE LUXURY OF GROWING OLD

THERE are certain advantages in growing old. The turbulence of youth is gone, with its quarrels, adolescent adjustments and secret tears. No need in maturity to explain oneself any more. One is accepted for what he is and as he is. As one grows older attitudes and values change. Instead of being eager to reform our fellow men we are more concerned to understand them. We cease to look for new friends, because the old and tested ones become dearer. An evening at home takes priority over a night

of friendly frivolity. One lives more in the present and less in the future. One suddenly sees new beauty in familiar things, a naked tree silhouetted against a fall sky, in shadows on the winter snow, in the outstretched arms of a child. Old age is not a time of life, it is a quality of mind.

TWO TOGETHER

HAVE you not seen from some vantage point the confluence of two great rivers? And have you remarked how one, like the rapid flowing Blue Nile, carries with it even to the delta far away much of the rich and muddy soil from the country through which it passes? Beside it moves the slower river from the plains, the White Nile, clear by comparison. Once joined together these two great rivers are distinguishable for miles as they flow side by side in the same river bed. They are separate yet united. So, too, when two separate yet loving hearts begin to live their lives together they may for some time go side by side, like two merged streams not fully united, yet the longer they stay together the more they have in common, continually losing some of their identity until they become as one. Each becomes an inseparable part of the other — as they become a family. Two people, husband and wife, may, like a river, later separate but the whole is diminished thereby and part of one goes with part of the other.

QUIET INSIDE

THE person who has learned to be content in whatever circumstances he finds himself is the one who knows how to live at peace with himself. Such a person is not upset because he does not win every contest. He finds his satisfaction in playing the game for the joy of playing, not for the victory. Such a person has thought through his sense of values so that the fulfillment of his desires brings inner satisfaction and peace of mind rather than unrest and remorse. True peace is as often found in resisting passions as in satisfying them. The danger lies not so much in what we want, as in wanting something simply to satisfy an unworthy desire. The person who is content with himself knows how to be quiet within.

DEALING WITH AN ADVERSARY

IT HURTS to have unkind and untrue things said about us and it is not always possible to counteract or correct such charges. The temptation is strong to deny or refute the statements but to do so only aggravates the situation. The best way to respond to derogatory remarks is to live in such a way that all men will know that they are false. What we *are* always speaks louder than any words which may be said against us. In the fourth century John Chrysostom advocated a way of overcoming our adversaries that is unsurpassed: Said he, "Let us astound them by our way of life. For this is the main battle: If we do not exhibit a life better than theirs, nothing is gained. . . . Let us win them by our life . . . for this is more powerful than the tongue." The best protection to reputation is to live above reproach.

LIKE SHADES AND STREAMS IN A DRY LAND

A MAN shall be "like a hiding place from the wind, a covert from the tempests, like streams of water in a dry place, like the shade of a great rock in a weary land." This ancient description of man is not some pious, over-idealistic goal which can never be achieved. It is a practical philosophy of life which stands as a challenge of what man ought to be and of what man can be! When life strips us bare of what was once held dear, when the towering shelter and comfort of some loved one has been taken away, when the very things to which we have given ourselves are destroyed, when life has become barren like a desert, then it is good to have a friend and to be a friend who will be as a river of water or as the shadow of a great rock in a weary land.

WHAT IS PRAYER?

IN THE Field Museum of Chicago there was an exhibit portraying life as it was lived in the Stone Age. The mother and children were sitting on a rock before a fire just outside a cave, while the father stood facing the east with arms outstretched to greet and pay homage to the rising sun. This was primitive man's way of recognizing his dependence upon some other worldly power. This salutation to the dawn was his form of prayer. Prayer assumes there is a Supreme Being, that this power which rules the universe, God, is concerned with our needs and desires, and that it is possible for us to approach God in the assurance He will hear us and help us. Prayer is not an attempt to change God's mind, but an attempt to let God change our minds. Prayer is an attempt to cooperate with the inexorable laws of the universe and to move in the direction God would have us go.

THE PRICE OF PRAYER

For what can we pray? Whatever is nearest and dearest to us, whatever weighs heaviest on our heart, belongs in our prayers provided it is in accord with God's will. Our finite minds cannot predict what is in God's infinite mind, but we can eliminate many requests which we know are unworthy. Earnest prayer, even for a definite object may set in motion forces which are as yet undiscovered or undetermined. Through prayer we may bring to pass things which would not otherwise be possible. We must, however, be willing to pay the price of having our prayers answered. One minister, for instance, prayed that someone from his parish might enter foreign service, but when his daughter decided to become a missionary he put every obstacle in her way that he could. The minister was unwilling to pay the price of having his prayers granted!

IN THE LIGHT OF THE ALTAR FIRE

IN ANCIENT days it was the duty of the solitary priest to go in darkness to the enclosure of the temple altar to clear away the ashes of the fire which was kept continually burning. It was the rule of the temple that he go in alone, that he carry no lamp, and that he walk in the light of the altar fire. To stand before the soft glow of dying embers and to be alone in a sanctuary is a soul-searching experience enabling one to see and feel things he never has before. It is good to take time to be holy and occasionally to walk in the light of the altar fire.

PURE DESIRES

AT TIMES we find ourselves doing what we do not want to do and failing to do what we ought to do, not because we do not know right from wrong, not because we are unconcerned, but because in spite of ourselves we are held in the grip of some power that controls our acts and decisions. This force is not so much one that drives us against our will as the fierce and steady winds bend the tree, as it is a force that pulls us, like the plant that is bent towards the light, in a direction we would not otherwise go. That which controls our responses in spite of our intentions, is deep-seated. This desire, — urge, ambition, temptation, passion — call it what you will, is the dominant, governing force of life. Desire, rather than intellectual judgment, controls most decisions. That is why it is imperative that our desires be noble and worthy. Only he who has pure motives will know the fullness of life.

ON GIVING

HE WHO strives to get all he can soon finds that he does not possess but that he himself is possessed. He is intent on getting not because he needs but because he wants. He who tries to save for himself all that he can, becomes not a benefactor but a miser. He builds bigger barns

to store his goods . . . for what purpose? He who gives all he can lives in a new dimension. The wise man uses his gifts as a trust and not a possession. Man is not the owner but the steward of his earthly goods. His time and abilities and possessions are a trust from God to be used for the benefit of mankind. Give and do not count the cost; give for the pure joy of giving.

BECAUSE WE MAY OR BECAUSE WE MUST?

COERCION conquers men outwardly but leaves them inwardly unsubdued. A wise leader uses a minimum of compulsion and a maximum of persuasion. Most people resent and resist doing things they have to do, just because somebody else wants them to do them, yet nothing will keep a person from doing the things he wants to do and which he believes ought to be done. That is why it is important that we see purpose in what is demanded of us and why that purpose must be worthy enough to command our best. Power and authority may compel, but such things as beauty, goodness, friendship, truth and love *invite!* The issues of life are in invitations which we may accept or reject. These invitations, when accepted, can save us from ourselves and fulfill our destiny.

RECONCILIATION

PROBABLY the greatest need of the world today is for reconciliation. In order to establish the proper relationship with others, we must be willing to admit our share of the responsibility and be willing to forgive. If we have been wronged, then we must be willing to forgive unconditionally, for partial forgiveness is not forgiveness at all. To admit our share of the guilt may not restore damage done, but it will reassure the other person that our motives are well intended. Admission of guilt and forgiveness are the twin foci around which reconciliation revolves.

THE COURAGE OF CONVICTIONS

ONE of life's great temptations is to yield to the popular side of an issue. When confronted with the prospect of standing firm and holding fast to a conviction at the cost of security, it is a temptation to compromise and to rationalize. Under pressure we often conclude that the cost is too great and the results too meagre to warrant the sacrifice. Indeed, it is often reasoned that the popular side is the winning side and that to follow the unpopular road of our inner convictions might place us on the losing side. The great leaders of the world have always been true to themselves and have had the courage of their convictions. Ultimate victory is on the side of right. The problem challenging us is not which side will win but how great a price are we willing to pay for our convictions?

GOOD INTENTIONS

It is difficult and at times impossible to tell what is the right and proper thing to do. By desiring the good, even when we do not quite know what it is, we tend to throw the influence of our weight on the side of righteousness and thereby become part of the power at work against evil. In this way we help to widen the circle of light and narrow the area of darkness. Our good intentions may, of course, prove to be wrong; but such errors are mistakes of judgment rather than of motive, and are more easily corrected. Motives and intentions are deep seated and their consequences are far-reaching, affecting innumerable individual and group decisions. That is why it is imperative that our purpose be pure and our intentions be good.

DEGREES OF GIVING

A Spanish scholar of the twelfth century, Moses Maimonides, depicts seven steps in what he calls the ladder of charity and giving: The first and lowest degree is to give, but with reluctance. The second is to give cheerfully, but not in proportion to the distress of the sufferer. The third step is to give cheerfully and proportionately, but not until solicited. The fourth is to give cheerfully, proportionately and unsolicitedly, but yourself to put the gift in the poor man's hand, thus exciting in him the painful emotion of shame. The fifth is to know the object of your bounty, but to remain unknown to him. The sixth is to bestow charity in such a way that the benefactor may not know the recipient, nor the recipient his benefactor. The seventh and worthiest step is to anticipate charity by preventing poverty. This is the highest step and the summit of charity's golden ladder.

TEMPTATIONS

WHEN Ulysses was sailing by the Isle of Sirens, he, according to legend, ordered wax put into the ears of the crew, then he had himself strapped to the mast, and the helm locked straight ahead so that they would not be lured from their course by the enchanting music of the Sirens. When Orpheus passed by he allegedly played so beautifully that the music of the Sirens held no appeal for his men. The strong are not shielded from temptation, but are they who have within sufficient strength of character to overcome temptations rather than be overcome by them. Every temptation is great or small according to one's ability to resist.

MISGUIDED LOVE

WE MAY be inclined to give everything to our children and to ask nothing in return. This may be an expression of genuine love, but in so doing we are actually teaching our children to expect everything and to give nothing. Children and parents need to understand that in the give-and-take of life both must do their share of giving. Love prompts us to shield our children from hardships and to conceal from them what is immoral, but such protection is unrealistic and of dubious value. True love does not spare one from hardships, but helps one to overcome them and conquer them. The child who is given everything never becomes the responsible, mature person he ought to be. The sheltered child, like the hot-house plant, is seldom able to withstand the rigors of later life. It is misguided love and not kindness to remove all obstacles.

TO YIELD OR TO RESIST?

MAN may not be able to create or to control the great forces that are at work around him, but he can learn to reckon with them, to resist or to yield, as exigencies demand. Just as the sailor cannot raise the wind or direct its course, but can put himself in the way of the great trade winds, resisting or yielding as circumstances warrant, so our response to situations will determine what we become. It is, indeed, the set of the sail and not the gale that determines our direction. In order to reach our destination against severe opposition we, like the skipper sailing against the wind, may need to tack and take a zig-zag course in order to make headway. Or, as in the game of Chinese checkers, we may need to move sideways and even backwards in order to move forward. The successful person is one who learns to make progress in spite of difficulties.

SHADE OR FRUIT?

WHEN an apple tree begins to run to wood and leaves, instead of fruit, the farmer severely crops it. Almost always, the tree begins to bear fruit. Why this should be, we do not know, but it is equally true that people whose lives seem to be purposeless may direct their energies toward more purposeful living once they have been wounded or hurt. Every branch in us that does not bear fruit should be cut off, and every branch that bears fruit should be pruned that it may bring forth more fruit. Too many people whose lives should be fruitful have developed

into shade trees. We sometimes try to protect ourselves too much. What we lose in flowers we may gain in fruit.

THE MOST PRICELESS POSSESSION

RELIGION says that the indefinable something known as the "soul" is the most precious thing in all the world. It is the soul which differentiates man from beast. To say that God breathed into man the breath of life and man became a living soul is an imaginative way of saying that there is something of God in every human being. To keep our identity with God alive, this most priceless possession must be nurtured. The great leaders of the world have urged the cultivation of the divine in man. God is a spirit and that is why we need to set our hopes in things spiritual rather than in worldly, material power.

GETTING ALONG WITH OTHERS

SCIENTISTS tell us that a lump of charcoal and a precious diamond are made of the same thing — carbon. The only difference between them is the arrangement of their atoms. Living together in harmony is also a matter of our relationship. It is a physical impossibility to be divorced completely from society and live completely isolated lives. This means that we must not only live with others but learn to get along with them. The kind of relationship we establish with those around us is basically a religious matter, for religion orients us, gives us a point of view, and determines what our attitude towards others will be. It will govern, for instance, whether we will seek to get what we can from the other person or whether we will try to do to others as we want them to do to us. Religion is not a way of looking at certain things but a certain way of looking at all things — our relationships, our differences, our misfortunes, our responsibilities, our rights, and our purposes.

RESTORING RELATIONSHIPS

A PERSON who has been wronged may suffer from heartache, from damage to reputation and from loss of property, yet if a right relationship is to be restored between the persons involved a still greater price may have to be paid by the injured party. It is usually the innocent person rather than the offender who has to pay an extra price if right relationships are to be restored. Restitution of material things may not always be possible but the restoring of friendship is possible and is always more important than possessions. Even though the injured may have to take the initiative and pay still heavier prices and sacrifices of time and patience and possessions, it is worth the cost.

MARRIAGE AND RELIGION

RELIGION is a most powerful and effective force in the building of a happy married life. Statistics show that the divorce rate is much lower among church-going people than among non-church-going people. It is not that these people are protected from the hazards, for they must face the same difficulties that others face with illness, in-laws, incompatibility, — but their religion, nurtured by regular Sabbath observance, builds into them qualities that enable them to hold together in times of adversity. Religion makes them more sensitive to the needs of others. Religion also regards marriage as a permanent, not a temporary or trial relationship. A happy and successful marriage demands that a couple stay together "for better or for worse, for richer for poorer, in sickness and in health, to love and to cherish," till death doth them part.

KEEPING OUR BALANCE

ONE of the circus acts which always fascinates an audience is the tight-rope walker. We admire the ability of anyone who can keep life under control and keep dangerous extremes and opposing forces in balance. Some people go to such extremes that their judgment is impaired and they become fanatics. Others are so overly cautious that they become ineffective and innocuous. Desirable as it is to keep on even keel and avoid excesses, one need not go to the other extreme of doing nothing or maintaining neutrality. The tight-rope walker can never just stand still. Like the bicycle rider, he must keep moving just to keep in balance. To keep a proper balance requires action, and if we would keep opposing forces in check we must constantly adjust to circumstances.

THE ETERNAL NOW

AMONG philosophers the present is known as "the moment." The present is all important because it is in that instant that we decide what the past shall mean to us and how the future shall take shape. Our use of "the moment," then, reflects our meaning of existence. For the person who believes himself to be the product of circumstances beyond his control, the present moment has lost significance and life has lost its purpose. Within our hands we hold all that is precious from the past. Through us all that is of value in the past will be transmitted to the future. We, of this generation, are the living link between the past and the future. We are the present.

POWER TO BECOME

TO CRITICIZE or to find fault with someone is to fail to see that person in his full possibilities. It is to see his many weaknesses rather than his many strengths. It is an attempt, albeit unconsciously and usually unsuccessfully, to get the other person to conform to our way of thinking.

This alienates. The irony is that the critic himself is usually the one who is blind. To accept people as they are and for what they are, to place confidence in them and to encourage them, is to help them become better than they are. To treat people as if they were what they ought to be is to help them to become what they are capable of becoming. Within every person is the capacity to become something greater than he now is. It is possible for each of us to become better and to help others to become what they ought to be.

SINNER OR SAINT?

THE pundit who remarked, "There is only one thing I can't resist—and that is temptation" understood human weakness and frailty. The person who yields to temptation, or who "misses the mark," soon becomes separated from God and is commonly called a sinner. A little child, overhearing adult conversation relating to one of the figures in the stained glass window of a cathedral, asked the adults if they meant "the man the light shines through?" That childish remark is an imaginative description of a saint—"a

man the light shines through." There are many who have not been sanctified by the church but whose lives exemplify such transparency, such clarity of purpose and sacrificial love that they are virtually saints. We become like what we love. It is possible for us to become better people than we now are, to become more saint-like, depending upon what we love.

TWO LOVING HEARTS

MARRIAGE is the bond that ties two loving hearts together. As each ministers to the other, stands by the other, complements as well as compliments the other, the relationship is made fast like the strands of a rope. Love does not consist of two people gazing fondly into each other's eyes but in moving together in the same direction. As the maple cannot grow under the shadow of the towering oak, so one helpmate cannot develop under the domination of the other. Husband and wife, like two musicians playing different notes on different instruments should be able to create harmony as the tones of one blend with those of the other.

LIVING BY GRACE

GRACE is doing for another being kindnesses he doesn't deserve, hasn't earned, could not ask for, and can't repay. Its main facets are beauty, kindness, gratitude, charm, favor, and thankfulness. Grace offers man what he cannot do for himself. The unwritten creed of many is that God is under obligation to them, but grace suggests that we are under obligation to God. To live in that consciousness is to live by grace. Living by grace is costly; it means sharing. It has no meaning apart from a spirit of self-sacrifice that prompts the soul to think more of giving than of receiving, of caring for others rather than for one's self.

LIVING VICARIOUSLY

SUFFERING becomes glorious when it is undertaken voluntarily, vicariously, and on behalf of another. Why this should be we do not know, but we do know that it is possible for evil to be used as a power for good, not just utilized for a good end. The process by which we can transform evil into good is by means of

vicarious suffering. If evil is going to be transmuted into good, then it must be done by someone doing something at his own expense which will benefit another and promote the sum total of goodness in the world. Sacrifice and vicarious suffering are processes through which evil may be converted into an instrument of goodness, but somebody must be willing to pay the price for such atonement.

TWO WORLDS

THERE is often conflict between the ideal and the practical, the remote and the immediate; and this conflict presents real problems. No simple formula will resolve these differences. We are asked to live according to idealistic, other-worldly standards and yet we must be judged by this world's practical standards. We are like the pilot who is air-borne yet earth-bound. As idealists we may live on a different plane and with a different set of standards than the pragmatist. The idealist will, for instance, regard love as a higher, broader basis of judgment than sheer retributive justice. He will seek to lay up treasures in heaven rather than upon

earth. He will measure values in terms of service to others rather than benefit to self. We need constantly to lift our sights above worldly standards, yet the extent to which we will respond to either of these contrasting situations will depend largely upon the pressures brought to bear, upon the strength of our courage and conviction, upon the clarity with which we see the issues.

BEREAVEMENT

DEATH does bring changes and adjustments for those who are left behind. The warmth and associations of former days are gone. The silence, the finality, the incommunicability disturb, but for the one who has triumphed there is rejoicing. Sorrow is centered more on self than on the deceased. One grieves, yet we would not want our grief taken from us, even if it could be, for our love is wrapped up with our grief. Grief is the price we pay for love. "Love is eternal, Death is a horizon, and the horizon is only the limit of our sight." It has been said, "Death is not extinguishing the light, but putting out the lamp because the dawn has come."